Appointment with Death

Stop Blaming Adam

Jackie Shaffer, Sr.

World rights reserved. This book or any portion thereof may not be copied or reproduced in any form or manner whatever, except as provided by law, without the written permission of the publisher, except by a reviewer who may quote brief passages in a review.

The author assumes full responsibility for the accuracy of all facts and quotations as cited in this book. The opinions expressed in this book are the author's personal views and interpretations, and do not necessarily reflect those of the publisher.

This book is provided with the understanding that the publisher is not engaged in giving spiritual, legal, medical, or other professional advice. If authoritative advice is needed, the reader should seek the counsel of a competent professional.

Copyright © 2018 Jackie Shaffer

Copyright © 2018 ASPECT Books

ISBN-13: 978-1-4796-0823-2 (Paperback)

ISBN-13: 978-1-4796-0824-9 (ePub)

Prior to Satan and sin, Adam had an appointment. I've got an appointment, and you've got an appointment with death—we all have an appointment with death (Hebrews 9:27). "Wherefore, as by one man sin entered into the world, and death by sin; and so death passed upon all men, for that all have sinned" (Romans 5:12). Adam's choice to join Satan in sin is the path that led to this impending engagement.

Table of Contents

Preface vii

ONE :
Appointment with Death 1

TWO :
Savored Wisdom 11

THREE :
Tithes and Offerings 17

Preface

Due to Adam's choice to take the fruit of the tree of the knowledge of good and evil as opposed to the tree of life (Genesis 2:9, 2:16–17, 3:9–12) he was tainted by death. As a result, everything dies. Nonetheless, Adam was merely an accessory after the fact; Satan brought sin to the universe and he, Adam, simply opened the gateway to this earth. Sin, the breaking of God's law, is the assailant that ultimately kills.

Aided by Adam, the crime of sin entered the sanctuary of life, stripping it, and brought death to all. Because of Adam's sin, we're all going to die. We are felons with him. Sin carries the penalty of death and each of us is deserving of death.

Branded accessories after the fact, we must, in order to avoid the penalty of death, disassociate ourselves from Adam, or, if you will, sin. If we fail to do so, it will be no longer due to Adam that we will die—it will be because of our own choices that we will die.

Could death have been averted? What would have been the outcome had Adam eaten first from the tree of life as opposed to the tree of the knowledge of good and evil? Furthermore, which tree was to Adam's advantage to eat from first? Though Adam was advised of God as to what tree to eat from, did God know what tree Adam would eat from first?

Amid the pages of this book you'll learn why Adam ate first from the forbidden tree. Like clay in the hands of the potter, you will get a sense of why God made us the way He did: "Nay but, O man, who art thou that repliest against God? Shall the thing formed say to him that formed it, Why hast thou made me thus?"

(Romans 9:20). You will embark upon a journey to truth that will boggle your mind, and stagger your imagination. Probing the mystery to these questions and answers that have puzzled us for so long, this book is going to take you on a tour through the corridors of truth, showing you things that you never imagined or even dreamed. Surely this lesson will satisfy the ever-wondering soul. Here we are granted a window into the supernatural that lets us now view a portion of the blueprint from the Master Builder.

Chapter One

Appointment with Death

"And as it is appointed unto men once to die, but after this the judgment" (Hebrews 9:27). Because it is appointed unto man once to die, we were made mortal for the primary purpose of death. However, we are subsequently to undergo a metamorphosis followed by a new birth—the advent of being born again. Therefore, our primary purpose is not death but life and we were simply made mortal for the purpose of death. We were not appointed based on our choice—death was inevitable because our choice only acted out that which was preordained.

This is revealed in scripture and later fulfilled in Christ, yet nonetheless many of us have yet to learn just what Adam's role was in this problem of sin and death. Alluding to the first man, we are part of Adam (one man representing many members) and were created to experience a second birth. As Jesus says, "Marvel not that I said unto thee, Ye must be born again" (John 3:7).

Adam, as the forerunner of mankind was made mortal; in choosing to eat the forbidden fruit he retained his mortality. Therefore, his life remained temporary because he did not choose the tree of life. He had access to both: "And out of the ground made the Lord God to grow every tree that is pleasant to the sight, and good for food; the tree of life also in the midst of the garden, and the tree of knowledge of good and evil" (Genesis 2:9). These two trees had everything to do with Adam's physical and spiritual outcomes.

By eating from the forbidden tree as opposed to the tree of life, he subjected himself to his own mortality.

Falling short of God's expectation for mankind, the first man, Adam, said "no" to the tree of life (Genesis 2:9, 16–17, 3:11–12), thus confining us to a momentary life of sin. Figuratively speaking, this left us in the state of a fruitless caterpillar, void of the characteristics to transcend its original state. However, the larva is appointed to change into the form of a butterfly, and subsequently we were and are to ascend to the form of spirit: "It is sown a natural body; it is raised a spiritual body. There is a natural body, and there is a spiritual body" (1 Corinthians 15:44). Without the second birth, without taking on the spiritual body, there is only death.

Now, having fallen short, man needed the second birth which required a second Adam. "For since by man came death, by man came also the resurrection of the dead. For as in Adam all die, even so in Christ shall all be made alive" (1 Corinthians 15:21–22). This speaks of Christ, who through His death, reinstituted God's original plan for our lives, where we are not just to undergo a spiritual awaking by the spirit, but literally a new birth (John 3:6–7).

To fulfill His Father's will regarding the first Adam, Jesus emerged on the world's scene. "Then said he, Lo, I come to do thy will, O God. He taketh away the first, that he may establish the second. By the which will we are sanctified through the offering of the body of Jesus Christ once for all" (Hebrews 10:9–10).

We, in the sin of Adam, are poised for the second birth. Adam is of the earth and therefore the temporary. However, when we receive the spirit of the second Man, we in the holiness of Christ, recipients of the second birth, which is heavenly and eternal (1 Corinthians 15:45–49), and at that point we will have reached our potential.

Perfection: In rejecting the tree of life, for the purpose of perfection the first Adam failed, thus leaving us in need of being born again. To live we as mortals must put on immortality (1 Corinthians 15:53). Because of this, many fault the first Adam instead of themselves for the fate (sin and death) that has befallen them, and rightly so for "death passed upon all men, for that all have sinned" (Romans 5:12). Nonetheless, can we rule out our own responsibility and continue to blame Adam for the doom that precedes us? Blameworthy, yes, but can Adam be held as a license for our personal actions and sins?

Much guilt has been heaped on Adam over the centuries in an effort to excuse our sin. After reading this message, you will no longer have Adam to blame for your destiny, for "ye shall know the truth, and the truth shall make you free" (John 8:32).

Designated: Due to Adam, as we travel on life's highway, death awaits us. It is appointed unto every man once to die. Adam's sin is the avenue by which we reach this impending appointment with death (Romans 5:12) and judgment that follows (Hebrews 9:27).

"No man has power over the spirit to hold on to his life in the day of death...and death will not let go of them that are given to it" (Ecclesiastes 8:8). Innocent, guilty, good morals, no morals, adults, infants, every nationality, rich or poor—there is no discrimination when it comes to death. We were given to death in that we are born mortal. However, with the aid of this message, I hope you will find a measure of consolation and strength for our forthcoming engagement. Also, I hope to aid understanding of why we must embark upon this unwelcome journey.

Mortal: Created mortal, genetically man is a biological organism formulated from dust made flesh (Genesis 2:7, 6:3). He is a candidate for the spirit, yet is resigned to the physical. Humans, as temporary objects, are subject to death and decay. "That which is born of the flesh is flesh; and that which is born of the Spirit is spirit" (John 3:6). Since we are made flesh our appointment with death is sealed, given that the body is what dies. "And as it is appointed unto men once to die, but after this the judgement: So Christ was once offered to bear the sins of many" (Hebrews 9:27–28).

Scheme: As God's crowning jewel of creation, man was meant to live and eat of the tree of life. However, amid the blight of sin the scheme of things is that we were born to live and then to die. This death thereafter is followed by a resurrection to judgment—a judgment to determine eternal life or eternal death (Revelation

20:11–15). To explain, life is the reinstatement of an eternal existence in a spiritual dimension, while death is the annihilation of life and our mortal spirit in the realm of hell. "Fear not them which kill the body, but are not able to kill the soul: but rather fear him which is able to destroy both soul and body in hell" (Matthews 10:28).

Our human body is the fusion of life and death. These elements in opposition to each other denote a choice each must make: "I have set before you life and death, blessing and cursing: therefore choose life, that both thou and thy seed may live" (Deuteronomy 30:19). The granting of choice to humanity denotes an essential obligation of the Creator to illustrate the spirit of fairness. Subsequently, this allows us, in who life and death weigh in the balance, to choose between these two courses.

In this way, the playing field is leveled; it excludes partiality. All have an equal foundation on which to base their decision, thus giving us a fair assessment of ourselves in regard to life and death. The reality of eternal life is that we must first experience death. For this purpose we might taste both for "it is appointed unto men once to die" (Hebrews 9:27).

Distinguish: We can use this as a metaphor to help us understand the choice we all have to make. God set before man in the person of Adam the tree of life and the tree of the knowledge of good and evil (Genesis 2:9). He had a choice between the two. The tree of life represents God (Proverbs 3:13–18, 8:14, 8:19), spirit (John 4:24), the law (Exodus 20: 1–17), and life (John 1:4), while the tree of the knowledge of good and evil denotes man/flesh/a double mind (Genesis 6:3), the natural (1 Corinthians 15:41–47), and death (Genesis 2:7, Ezekiel 18:20). As the Bible says in the book of James, "For let not that man think that he shall receive any thing of the Lord. A double minded man is unstable in all his ways" (1:7–8). Galatians 5:19–21 further describes the evil fruits of a tree that are characteristic of man.

In all respect of choice, God gave Adam both trees but advised him to eat only of the tree of life (Genesis 2:16–17). Nonetheless, in recognition of man's choice involving the tree of life and the tree of the knowledge of good and evil, it was God's will for man that none should perish (2 Peter 3:9). However, God knew that man would eat of the tree of the knowledge of good and evil from the start, because He is all knowing. "O lord, thou hast searched me, and known me" (Psalm 139:1).

True to our human form, Adam's fleshly desire was for the fruit of the tree of the knowledge of good and evil. This stands in opposition to God and the tree of life. The natural flesh was in opposition to the spirit and it was only normal that Adam would yield to the natural.

Though he was commanded to eat from the tree of life, Adam was flesh and subject to the material realm. Adam's appetite craved the tangible, mentally and physically. He did not grasp how a piece of fruit could be so intertwined with the spirit. He had to learn: "It is written in the prophets, And they shall be all taught of God" (John 6:45). Through this act he learned that "For as the body without the spirit is dead" (James 2:26).

Purposely: Created mortal Adam was made subject to vanity in hope: "For the creature was made subject to vanity, not willingly, but by reason of him who hath subjected the same in hope" (Romans 8:20). Self-centered (an attribute of vanity) and territorial, Adam, as a child of the natural, did not and was not going to first eat from the tree of life. Yielding to vanity subjected Adam to the creative brilliance of God's love. As a result, man locked in his fate, ultimately affirming death in himself.

Anticipating this act (attesting to the blueprint of the Master Builder) God, being conscious of all things, allowed Adam to blunder. Consequently, He "Who in times past suffered all nations to walk in their own ways" (Acts 14:16). This was given that we (Adam) might come to see the error of our way (choice). "That they should seek the Lord, if haply they might feel after him, and find him, though he be not far from every one of us: For in him we live, and move, and have our being" (Acts 17:27–28).

Though subject to sin, we might live again, because God attentively allowed us to go the wrong way and in turn go the right way. This tells us it wasn't to man's advantage to first partake of the tree of life. Had he first eaten of the tree of life, he would have never focused solely on himself in opposition to God. He would have never known himself as who he is without God. Had he first partaken of the tree of life, which embodied God, he would have thought himself to be equal with God as did Satan, who said "I will ascend above the heights of the clouds; I will be like the most High" (Isaiah 14:14).

His opposition to first partaking of the tree of life distinguished man from God. Except for man's first choice—eating of the tree of the knowledge of good and evil—he would have never known separation from God. He would have never known disorder, affliction, sickness, disease, pain, suffering, or sorrow. Moreover, he would have never known death, which helps us appreciate our love for life.

Without suffering followed ultimately by death, we would never look to God as our Sustainer. On our way to God, we have an appointment with death. The glory it will produce out-weighs the pain it causes. The end result is something more than you can ask for or imagine.

We don't have to fear death; death belongs to us. It is a gift (ultimate grief) planned to help us reach our ultimate potential (eternal life). "Therefore let no man glory in men. For all things are your's; Whether Paul, or Apollos, or Cephas, or the world, or life, or death, or things present, or things to come; all are your's; And ye are Christ's; and Christ is God's" (1 Corinthians 3:21–23).

Regardless of one's relationship, occupation, or reputation, no matter how often we experience death, we never get used to it. The reason for this is we are not supposed to, given that God created us to live and the purpose of life is living. Appealing to life, God said in Deuteronomy 30:19, "Choose life and live."

Over looked: There was a time that God overlooked our ignorance: "And the times of this ignorance God winked at; but now commandeth all men every where to repent" (Acts 17:30). He permitted Adam (man) to venture out according to his own understanding. Yet He desires to be acknowledged; He attests to His existence as our Overseer. He gives us rain from heaven, fruitful seasons, and fills our hearts with gladness (Acts 14:16–17). He determines the time before the appointed end (death), and the "bounds of our habitation" (length of deration of life) (Acts 17:26). He also tells us how we are to conduct ourselves in life pertaining to the law (Exodus 20:1–17).

Now, man, one with Adam through the flesh, could not keep the law (illustrated by the rejection of the tree of life). To this end, our appointment with death was sealed, for the law is spiritual, and we are now but carnal flesh (Romans 7:14).

However, thus determined in advance, God predestined Christ, who is the fusion of humanity and deity into an individual and eternal oneness, to keep the law on our behalf to ensure our redemption. "But unto every one of us is given grace according to the measure of the gift of Christ" (Ephesians 1:7).

Christ in the flesh yet being the embodiment of spirit, was born under the law. He was subjected to its ordinance (regulations) in order to demonstrate our destiny. Because it is appointed to man once to die, Christ died once for us all (Hebrews 9:27). His sacrifice of the flesh, as it gives way to spiritual life, blossomed in a resurrection (1 Corinthians 15:40–45).

The spirit allows us to fully submit to God. "But ye shall receive power, after that the Holy Ghost [Spirit] is come upon you: and ye shall be witnesses unto me both in Jerusalem, and in all Judaea, and in Samaria, and unto the uttermost part of the earth" (Acts 1:8). Therefore, without the Holy Spirit, Adam could not submit to the tree of life. With the receiving of the Holy Spirit (symbolized in the tree of life), Adam, the embodiment of flesh, would have been empowered to submit to God, thereby, sacrificing the flesh in turn to receive a spirit filled glorified body reproduced in a resurrection.

Without the spirit, because of Adam's choice, man was simply left with a body gasping its last breath. God's choice opposed to Adam's offered gain. Here death becomes an asset rather than a liability, in that the flesh gives way to spirit resulting in a new birth. For this reason, we have an appointment with death. As the saying goes, "weeping is but for a moment but joy comes in the morning" (Psalms 30:5).

It is spirit— the Holy Spirit—that gets us from this life to life everlasting. By way of his choice Adam was alone, thus causing God to ask in Genesis 3:9, "Adam where are you?" Separated from God, Adam was by himself, hypothetically a dead man, in the world without God and without hope.

Ultimately death is the divide that separates true value from counterfeit value. Had Adam eaten first from the tree of life he would not have experienced death. The eyes of his understanding would not have been opened as to seeing or doing things his own way. Neither would he have effectively acquired an acute awareness of his personal existence independent of God. "And the eyes of them both were opened, and they knew that they were naked" (Genesis 3:7). Adam without his Creator was the equivalent of death. Death is the medium that brings us before ourselves; it elevates our consciousness and causes us to reflect on our mortality.

Adam was the fusion of humanity. Collectively, he embodied the human race. A solitary act by this one man, in whose loins resided all men, gave all men an unregenerate nature that had to be morally and spiritually regenerated by the Holy spirit. United in Adam, humanity sinned, at which point death entered the sanctuary of life—"Wherefore, as by one man sin entered into the world, and death by sin; and so death passed upon all men, for that all have sinned" (Romans 5:12).

Advocate of experience: Since it is appointed to man once to die, death comes to us all. Death unearths the fact that we don't possess inherent life, thus exposing our need for God. Jesus said of himself, "Search the scriptures; for in them ye think ye have eternal life: and they are they which testify of me" (John 5:39). As such, we are not immortal. Eternal life resides in, of, and with God, and not with us.

In the arena of his choice, Adam's attitude or demeanor was not that of animosity, enmity, hatred, disrespect or rebellion. The enormity of these thoughts only becomes roused after we come to the knowledge of the truth. "What shall we say then? Is the law sin?

God forbid. Nay, I had not known sin, but by the law: for I had not known lust, except the law had said, Thou shalt not covet" (Romans 7:7). Adam, also representing us, responded within the confines of his biological makeup and simply did what came naturally (Ephesians 2:3). Adam had yet to know he had sinned, "For until the law sin was in the world: but sin is not imputed when there is no law" (Romans 5:13). "Nevertheless death reigned from Adam to Moses, even over them that had not sinned after the similitude of Adam's transgression, who is the figure of him that was to come" (Romans 5:14).

Intelligent creatures blessed with the ability to think, flanked by God's law, makes man personally accountable. As was Adam (flesh), so are we. Confronted with the same choice Adam had, we must choose between flesh and spirit. Through the gift of choice, God allowed Adam to fail, and in turn we fail, so that we might come full circle with ourselves. Coming to terms with who and what we are—opposed to spirit—shapes humility.

We, like Adam, are independent entities, the crowning jewel of creation, biological organisms capable of reproducing multiple Adams, all given the same choice. Yet we are one, making us and us alone personally accountable for our own actions. Adam made an independent choice, making him and him alone accountable. Nonetheless, due to our biological ties—the avenue by which sin and death comes to everyone—Adam's personal choice affected us all. As such, we have a rendezvous with death. This does not mean that we are condemned to everlasting death, but, for the purpose of eternal life, we have a date with fatality.

Our fate does not rest upon what Adam did. Adam made his choice, and he now stands at the mercy of a God who gave him a second chance, a second judgment, where if found unrepentant, would carry the penalty of the second death (Revelation 20:11–15). "Blessed and holy is he that hath part in the first resurrection: on such the second death hath no power, but they shall be priests of God and of Christ, and shall reign with him a thousand years" (Revelation 20:6). May you be among these blessed souls. But that's another chapter, and your choice decides your fate. Will it be the tree of life and God, or the tree of the knowledge a of good and evil and the lust of the flesh? It is your choice, and you alone shall bear the consequences. Amen.

Chapter Two

Savored Wisdom

1. If you don't have your best interest at heart, then who does?
2. Your past doesn't define you; your future is whatever you want it to be.
3. God within us at our core is the best version of ourselves.
4. Love makes allowance for people's weakness.
5. Don't control people—empower them.
6. The ability to connect with other people is what's important.
7. Respectable communication requires listening.
8. Worry adds no value to our life; it's like sitting in a rocking chair where you're constantly moving but going nowhere.
9. If one dream dies, dream another dream.
10. Change the way you think and you'll change the way you are.
11. Stop saying things that subtract from your life.
12. Every day you live discouraged is a day wasted.
13. Let no one steal your joy.
14. What you water will grow.
15. It's not how you get there, it's who you become along the way.

16. It's not how you live, it's how well you live.
17. Ask no one for anything who do not have the power to do it.
18. If you're unhappy today is it because of something you want and don't have?
19. Your breakthrough is on the way.
20. It is not the size of the dog in the fight but the size of the fight in the dog.
21. God's grace is sufficient for the void we have in our lives.
22. Make room for God in your life and He will fill your life with good things.
23. What people do or don't do does not determine your worth.
24. If people don't want to be your friend, it's their loss and not yours.
25. When you run from one thing you will run from everything.
26. Remember David. Be a giant killer.
27. Tradition, as opposed to that which is new, welcomes you.
28. Transformation walks right upon you and challenges you to come.
29. Don't let a moment leave you stuck for life.
30. Time is our currency—use it wisely.
31. God will make you grab something you're scared of.
32. Embrace the serpent (trial and tribulation)—it is your rod.
33. God is not breaking us—He is making us.
34. Take off fear and put on courage.
35. What you do when nobody is looking is who you really are.

Savored Wisdom

36. Be yourself if you want people to love you.
37. Watch in your life who stays and who goes.
38. Know who you are—if you don't, people will define you.
39. That which is new requires advancing beyond.
40. If you want something new, something old has to die.
41. You don't put new wine in old bottles.
42. Pain introduces us to ourselves.
43. A broken heart is God's platform for greatness.
44. It is not the puppet on the stage but the puppet master behind the curtain.
45. Prioritizes your convictions.
46. Keep God involved lest the world swallow you up.
47. Who you are is not what you are.
48. If you know who you are then you know who you are not.
49. Your worth does not come from another person—it comes from your Creator.
50. You don't get over things—you get through them and keep moving forward.
51. When a butterfly leaves it's cocoon it never goes back.
52. Go with the living.
53. Sit not among them that are dead while they live.
54. Don't be suspended in life, going forward while engaging in hindsight.
55. Remember Lot's wife.
56. Caring too much about the things of this world will choke you to death.
57. Keep your altitude.
58. Everything that goes can't stay and everything that stays can't go.

59. Stand still and see the salvation of God.
60. It is good when people validate you, but don't depend on that.
61. If you know the combination you can get into anything.
62. The only power people have over you is the power you give them.
63. Teamwork make a dream work.
64. Smile at somebody.
65. Pursue love.
66. Amid asking for a blessing be a blessing.
67. You don't have to show it, you don't have to flash it, just be it.
68. Don't get to the end of the day having no fruit—nothing good to show for it.
69. God called us to be fruitful—productive.
70. Fear causes you to freeze.
71. Fear only attacks what you are afraid to lose.
72. If you are already on the plane, you might as well enjoy the ride.
73. We learn obedience through the things we suffer.
74. If you are under attack, there is something to be gained.
75. When something is certain there is nothing to be brave about.
76. People judge you by what you say and do.
77. People don't remember you by what you say and do, they remember you based on how they feel about you.
78. Where you are going is more important than were you've been.
79. If there is something you wanted and didn't get it, you didn't need it.

80. You may not kill a thought but you can stop the thought from killing you.
81. When a person goes to jail he is not destroyed, just brought under control.
82. Anything you have to have is out of balance.
83. Don't lose the real over the imaginary.
84. The giver is always better than the gift.
85. It is with the mind we serve the Lord.
86. Let people off the hook—they can't give you what they don't have.
87. Give people room to be who they are.
88. People believe when you believe.
89. In order for people to follow, you must feed them; take them to the next level.
90. You listen to yourself more than anyone else, so be careful of what you say to yourself.
91. Don't leave the one that blesses for the blessing.
92. Quit letting the accuser tell you who you are.
93. You don't seduce what you already have.
94. Do something that will make you laugh.
95. Yesterday is gone; we won't be back that way again.
96. We live one day at a time.
97. Yesterday's manna doesn't suffice for today. A new day requires regathering of nourishment.
98. Consult with the Lord; don't just sample the bread.
99. Seeing and not recognizing—that is man's weakness and Satan strength.
100. Today God may say strike the rock and tomorrow speak to the rock.
101. We are not to rely on formality.

102. A fool will lose tomorrow looking back on yesterday.
103. Live today in the hope of tomorrow.
104. Learn from yesterday.
105. Love, joy, and peace, these are the desires of a man's heart.
106. We know where we've been but we can't say where we're going.
107. "The fear of the Lord is the beginning of wisdom." The moment you reverence God, humble yourselves in acknowledgement of who He is, is the moment you attain true intellect. Wisdom is His; He is understanding.
108. Life is a gift no matter what's handed down; if you've been dealt a bad hand, it is up to you how you play it.
109. Life is a feast—even the crumbs that fall from the table.
110. Life moves fast—if you don't stop and look around you could miss it.
111. Success is the fulfillment of duty.
112. The hen never catcalls until the egg is laid.
113. I've met the enemy—it is me—I'm my worst rival.
114. Be nervous, be afraid, for fear causes you to save yourself.
115. If you think something is impossible, then for you it is.

Chapter Three

Tithes and Offerings

"Will a man rob God? Yet ye have robbed me. But ye say, Wherein have we robbed thee? In tithes and offerings. Ye are cursed with a curse: for ye have robbed me, even this whole nation. Bring ye all the tithes into the storehouse, that there may be meat in mine house, and prove me now herewith, saith the Lord of hosts, if I will not open you the windows of heaven, and pour you out a blessing, that there shall not be room enough to receive it" (Malachi 3:8–10).

Subsequently, we will branch out to other worlds: the restoration and colonizing of the cosmos. We are going to occupy, among other things, uninhabited, dead, dilapidated planets, mansions, if you will, or, vacant hotels. These are worlds without end, where we shall reign and rule with Christ throughout the universe. "If we suffer, we shall also reign with him: if we deny him, he also will deny us" (2 Timothy 2:12). By way of the cross, Christ prepared the way, for "In my Father's house are many mansions: if it were not so, I would have told you. I go to prepare a place for you. And if I go and prepare a place for you, I will come again, and receive you unto myself; that where I am, there ye may be also" (John 14:2–3).

Please notice, God did not say, "Bring all the tithes, and offerings into the storehouse," but rather, "bring all the tithes into the storehouse." The word "bring" and "offerings" are similar in meaning and therewith denotes the same purpose. We've robbed God in that we have not presented that which results in an offering.

The bringing of the tithes brings about the offering: "Thus ye also shall offer an heave offering unto the Lord of all your tithes, which ye receive of the children of Israel" (Numbers 18:28). According to Leviticus 27:32, "And concerning the tithe of the herd, or of the flock, even of whatsoever passeth under the rod, the tenth shall be holy unto the Lord." Synonymous of one another, tithes are giving a tenth of the proceeds; offerings are the giving of the proceeds. With the introduction of this revelation let us now proceed to unlock this unsettling mystery.

Before we can begin to understand the gravity of Malachi 3:8–10, we must first acquire an understanding of what tithes and offerings are. Only then we can begin to comprehend the significance of the demand. Acceptance with understanding makes room for tolerance, therefore freeing us to give. That being said, let us now break the yoke that makes us so resentful when it comes to tithing.

Drawing from Matthew 26:34–35, Jesus said unto Peter, "Verily I say unto thee, That this night [denoting spiritual darkness] before the cock crow [denoting spiritual enlightenment], thou shalt deny me thrice." Then Peter said to Jesus, "Though I should die with thee, yet will I not deny thee. Likewise also said all the disciples."

After that a multitude came out against Jesus, at which time all the disciples forsook him, and fled; and all that laid hands on Jesus led him away to the high priest's palace, but Peter followed him a far off and went in with the servant, to see the end. In the course of events the chief priest's and elders, and all of the council, sought false witnesses against Jesus, to put him to death. "Then did they spit in his face, and buffeted him; and others smote him with the palms of their hands" (Matthew 26:67).

As Peter sat within the palace, two maids and they that stood by, said unto him, "Thou also wast with Jesus of Galilee...Surely thou also art one of them" (Matthew 26:69, 73). In the wake of blame, Peter denied all three accusations, cursing and swearing, saying "I do not know the man", and immediately the cock crowed. Remembering the words of Jesus, "Before the cock crow, thou shalt deny me thrice," (Matthew 26:34) and conceding the denial, "he went out, and wept bitterly" (Matthew 26:75). With the support of these scriptures we shall clarify what it is we've robbed God of, in the hope of making good that which is due Him.

To rob is to by unlawful means seize and carry off the property of another. This denotes any object a person may lawfully attain to and or hold. To rob is to deny or deprive someone of something belonging to or due them. As a disciple of Christ, Peter's denial caused God to suffer a duel loss. Peter and all that was to be done on his behalf—personal commitment alternating with what he had to offer—was gone.

We contribute among the diversities of our assets what we have attained. Whether mental, physical, spiritual, or material, we give of our belongings what we can afford. Coinciding with this concept, please note Peter's response to a beggar: "Silver and gold have I none; but such as I have give I thee: In the name of Jesus Christ of Nazareth rise up and walk" (Acts 3:6). Peter exemplified the spirit of giving found in the Bible: "Every man according as he purposeth in his heart, so let him give; not grudgingly, or of necessity: for God loveth a cheerful giver" (2 Corinthians 9:7). When it comes to tithing, Peter, having not "silver or gold," makes null and void the offering being a distinct commodity such as money. Armed with this revelation we can now began to differentiate between what belong and what was taken.

"Now the body is not for fornication, but for the Lord; and the Lord for the body" (1 Corinthians 6:13). Originally, prior to being saved or unsaved, "your body is the temple of the Holy Ghost [God is the architect of our existence] which is in you [It is His Spirit that generates life in us], which ye have of God, and ye are not your own" (1 Corinthians 6:19).

Even though our bodies are the temple of the Holy Spirit, it does not mean we are holy. We are not holy, neither do we innately have the Holy Spirit such as a child of God; that spirit must be received. The spirit spoken of is the attribute of God's spirit giving fullness to life. It enables us to live, reason, comprehend, and exercise thoughts and emotions. The knowledge, or if you will, scheme, to our existence resides in Him. "For in him we live, and move, and have our being" (Acts 17:28). "For by him were all things created, that are in heaven, and that are in earth, visible and invisible, whether they be thrones, or dominions, or principalities, or powers: all things were created by him, and for him" (Colossians 1:16).

Denoting prior claim to ownership, God is Creator, Owner, and Proprietor of everything we see and don't see. We ourselves are a tithe and offering to God. Note the following: "The earth is the Lords and the fullness thereof the world and they that dwell therein" (Psalm 24:1). In light of Peter's denial, where was God robbed in regard to tithes and offerings? Let it be said, tithes are the proceeds, and the proceeds are the harvest, or the amount of goods deriving from work, land, livestock, industry, or as previously noted in Leviticus 27:32, "whatsoever passeth under the rod, the tenth shall be holy unto the Lord."

Drawing from work, land, livestock, or industry, tithes originate in the form of money, crops, animals, steel, oil, gas, etc. Essentially tithes come from the field of a man's possessions, or that which he has acquired and owns, himself included, seeing we have acquired and are in possession of ourselves.

All things and all people derive from God. He has given us life, and the proceeds deriving from life is the living. We owe God our lives. Obligated, we are to submit to Him in acknowledgement of His lordship and dominion.

In comparing ourselves to merchandise, we are His primary treasure. Overall, in terms of goods, we ourselves are the tithes in reference to God's claim. Among all else, it is we God produced in terms of earnings. We are His capital. Similar to assets, we as a person are the tool God utilizes to invest in His church. Surely God can have even the stones serve him: "that God is able of these stones to raise up children unto Abraham" (Matthew 3:9). He can use anything but He chose us. For lack of this knowledge we are under a curse.

Now, regarding what we produce and earn, as a contribution, that is what we use to invest in the church. The Old Testament, the embodiment of the law, deemed it mandatory to give a precise ten percent as tithe (Leviticus 27:32). However, regarding obligation, this merely emphasizes the importance of giving. Giving is the general order of life. Life emanates in, of, and around giving. Life breeds life, as rain waters seed and seed yields fruit. Sowing and reaping are the order designed into our world.

We are no longer under the Old Testament, which catered to bondage, where a man was required to give of his assets based on a fixed sum at a given point and time. In contrast, we should be compelled by sincerity that is yet consistent with a personal obligation to give freely as opposed to a mandatory percentage. According to the New Testament, "Every man according as he purposeth in his heart, so let him give; not grudgingly, or of necessity: for God loveth a cheerful giver" (2 Corinthians 9:7).

Now, as opposed to a tenth, as His people, God requires 100% of our hearts. This is not simply goods—this involves self-service, the offering up of oneself as a sacrifice in service of our faith. We are told to "present your bodies a living sacrifice, holy, acceptable unto God, which is your reasonable service" (Romans 12:1). In conjunction with material things, it is contrary to offering up oneself in service to God to lay siege to and carry off the property of that which belong to and is due Him, chiefly, ourselves.

Now, the giving of that which is to be received denotes an offering. According to Numbers 18:26, "When ye take of the children of Israel the tithes which I have given you from them for your inheritance, then ye shall offer up an heave offering of it for the Lord, even a tenth part of the tithe." Notice this verse equate offering with tithe. Though commanded, the giving of offerings, spiritual in essence, involves an act of the will, a decision to give of our assets. Opposed to two duties, giving a tithe followed by an offering contradicts scripture since tithes constitutes the offering. Now, there is a diversity of offerings, such as peace offerings, sin offerings, heaven offering, etc. Still, tithes make up the offerings where we offer up what we've received on behalf of God in conjunction with a given ceremony (Numbers 18:28).

Seeing an offering relative to tithes, we rob God by not giving or sharing with Him what He has given us. As noted, tithes are the goods; an offering is a decision whereof we decide to give of our goods. We've robbed God of the tangible, ourselves instead of things, and we've robbed Him of our will. If our will aligns with His will, us along with our belongings depicts the practice of tithing.

Seeing this, we have robbed God of His primary source of treasure—ourselves. Having ascertained God has no pleasure in sacrifice without oneself; we find the soul giving of his or her life in total obedience followed by the sharing of one's possessions consummates in acceptance. Therefore, when God says, "Bring all the tithes into the storehouse," we see a dual representation. The building in which one stores up commodities coincides with a building God is referring to as His people.

Both are depicted by a building. One is a material storehouse for treasure but it represents something more. Corresponding to this building, we as God's people are to build upon Christ: "upon this rock I will build my church" (Matthew 16:18). We as a people are the recipients of God's demand. Let it be noted that the building is not the purpose—the purpose is in the building. For lack of this this knowledge we are under a curse.

Finding the word church to be twofold in scripture, we must differentiate between a structure and a people. Similar to a building, to our amazement, we as people find we also are the house of God. Together, we are a place of refuge when we gather on one accord.

The gather together with one another denotes unity in the body of Christ. Similar to a building, we are the storehouse. As a subject of God's house, we along with our goods are a unit. Therefore, we give of our goods in union with ourselves. This denotes unconditional surrender, where one totally yields his or her life in service to God. In this way, the giving of things in union with oneself relative to the church becomes a way of life: the giving is always flowing outward. For like of this knowledge we are under a curse.

As a sanctuary, the body of Christ is to receive and store up for further use of the band of believers. Hand in hand to bringing all the tithes into the storehouse is to win over souls, preach (confront the masses), teach (grant understanding), and provide (edify). The church is the depository of the converted, a place of safekeeping, where the unsaved have become saved. It is a place of assembly where all amass in one accord.

The inward flow of believers denotes food in God's house. Jesus is the bread of life (John 6:35), and we are the body of Christ, subsequently bread for food. We are His host, ministers of his that do his pleasure: "Bless ye the Lord, all ye his hosts; ye ministers of his, that do his pleasure" (Psalms 103:21). As occupants in God's house, we sow seed. The seeds that are scattered, or placed, represent the Word of God introduced or implanted into the hearts of men. The sower noted as the saint, dispenses the word (Mattew13:18–23).

Now, the seed that are sown denotes the preaching of the gospel, "the word of the kingdom" (Matthew 13:19). Seeds result in growth (Matthew 13:23). The increase of believers joining to the body of Christ satisfies the cry for food in God's house. In terms of God's house, we are the nourishment of which He speaks. As food nourishes, in proclaiming the gospel, we feed the masses. As residents of God's house, one plants (preach), another waters (teach), but God causes the increase (growth). "Who then is Paul, and who is Apollos, but ministers by whom ye believed, even as the Lord gave to every man? I have planted, Apollos watered; but God gave the increase" (1 Corinthians 3:5–6).

God admonishes us to follow up on tithes and offering (the offering up of oneself in turn with his or her possessions), and witness the results of a transcendent blessing. Moreover, He admonishes us to test Him in this and prove the accuracy of that which He has affirmed. That there be no doubt, through ministry, God subjected Himself to judgment before the finite. Through this sacrifice, the people acknowledged and glorified God. Public testimony, shown in demonstration of their faith due to the liberal distribution of the gospel, bore witness to all men of the authenticity of God's word.

Through the administration of the gospel, its profound effect and perceived life changing power observed by the people, many may enter and therewith become one with the household of God. Subjection upon reception of the gospel fills God's house, ultimately opening the flood gates of heaven, whereafter the praises go up and the blessing come down. "Blessed be the God and Father of our Lord Jesus Christ, who hath blessed us with all spiritual blessings in heavenly places in Christ" (Ephesians 1:3).

God compels humanity to come together in unity. As a tithe, have you given yourself and your possessions over to God? Or have you robbed God of His church by holding back yourself from His storehouse? Amen.

Prior to this revelation, I found myself resentful when tithes were called for, though I believed tithes were a divine command as well as a basic necessity. Heaven addressed my lack of resolve, and this message makes it easier for me to give of my assets, since the focal point isn't my possession, but me in conjunction with my belonging. On behalf of the gospel, in accordance with freewill, I ascertained as I have freely received of God, even so, I should freely give, bearing in mind to give what is adequate according to my economic status. Amen.

We invite you to view the complete
selection of titles we publish at:
www.ASPECTBooks.com

We encourage you to write us
with your thoughts about this,
or any other book we publish at:
info@ASPECTBooks.com

ASPECT Books' titles may be purchased in
bulk quantities for educational, fund-raising,
business, or promotional use.
bulksales@ASPECTBooks.com

Finally, if you are interested in seeing
your own book in print, please contact us at:
publishing@ASPECTBooks.com
We are happy to review your manuscript at no charge.

www.ingramcontent.com/pod-product-compliance
Lightning Source LLC
Chambersburg PA
CBHW071752090426
42738CB00011B/2664